INCESSANT PAIN

Sometimes the pain is not understood but
you live with it anyways...

FARHA SHIREEN

Made with ❤ on the BookLeaf Publishing Platform
www.bookleafpub.in
www.bookleafpub.com

Dedication

To my beloved—
without whom the pain was inevitable,
and this story, perhaps, unavoidable.

And to every soul who has ever carried the weight of a
broken heart—
may you find solace in knowing you are not alone.

Preface

Have you ever felt a pain with no memory attached—no words to recall, no face to remember—just a lingering ache left behind by someone?
It's a sharp, stinging pain that still lives within me.
A pain that seems less like a memory and more like a shadow of the heart—a quiet reflection of emotions one is forced to endure. It is the inevitable melancholy of my life.
This book is about that pain—how it took root, how it changed over time, and how it grew into something far more complex than I ever imagined.
These pages hold a piece of my life, written during one of the darkest and most difficult phases I've ever known. A part of me I never thought I'd share with anyone.
Because I'm not a writer.
And I still don't know if these words can truly capture the depth of heartbreak I experienced or the raw essence of what I felt.
But they are honest. And they are mine.

Acknowledgements

I couldn't be more grateful for this life and the blessing of having parents and brothers like mine. Your unconditional love, quiet strength, and constant presence have shaped who I am in ways I can never fully put into words.
Without your sacrifices, encouragement, and unwavering support, I wouldn't have made it through the storms that life brought my way. You stood by me when things were uncertain, and your belief in me became my anchor.

To my beloved husband— I am endlessly thankful to walk this path with you.

And to my dear friends—I have very few friends and they are very dear to me.Thank you all for bearing me for all these years.

This book is a piece of my heart, shaped and supported by the incredible people in my life.

With all my love and gratitude I am thankful to Almighty.

1. My Dear Pain

Oh, my dear pain,
Let no one ever see the weight you hold,
Wrap yourself in the memories, both bitter and bold.

Let no one ever pry into the depths of my scars,
You are the echo of battles fought with silent wars.

Oh, my dear pain,
Let no one ever see if you exist
conceal yourself in my silence
Guard your secrets well,
Woven in the fabric of my heart's shell.

Let no one ever ask if I am hurt
comfort yourself in my solitude
I promise to embrace you with my tears
you promise to preserve my integrity

Oh, my dear pain,

Let no one ever know if you make me weak
Pretend yourself in my strengths

Let no one ever question If you make my past
Fade yourself in my stories

Oh, my dear, pain
Let no one ever know you
As I have known you.....

2. House of Regrets

I wish a thousand knives could pass through me to
compensate the regret I'm in.
I wish a path of thorns lead me out of this,
Or an ounce of poison relieve me from the regret I'm in,
I wish there were a medicine to cure,
I wish the most viable option had been like nothing ever
happened at all.
I wish I could have gone back and choose better,
I wish I couldn't have come back to the house of regrets.
I wish......
I so wish......

3. Remembering

Remembering that enormous degree of pain that I could
not bear,
I went numb,
Not a tear rolled down,
broken and collapsed within,
Yet no one heard me,
Everything was transcending in silence.....

4. Melancholy of Pain

It wasn't about the choice to part,
It wasn't about the love they shared,
It was all about the memories that,
Haunted her in the depths of Pain.

It wasn't about who left,
It wasn't about who stayed,
It was simply about the pursuit,
the pursuit of love,
that left her in the melancholy of Pain.....

It was about what was right,
it was about what was wrong,
It was about what he did to her,
that left her in the melancholy of Pain......

It wasn't about how much she wanted him,
It wasn't about how much he wanted her,
It was all about the destiny,
A destiny that left her in the melancholy of Pain.....

It wasn't about who won,
It wasn't about who lost,
It was all about loosing each other,
that left her in the melancholy of Pain.....

It wasn't about forgiving,
It wasn't about forgetting,
it was all about finding someone else,
that left her in the melancholy of Pain.........

5. Rescue

Surrounded by unwavering pain,
Guiding her through the shadows' embrace,
Painting light on the walls of despair,
Flickering hope in vastness.

Her abode was captivated in darkness,
Until stars came to her rescue.......

6. Neither

Neither in Love
Neither in Pain
Neither did she choose herself
Neither did she choose him
She decided to die somewhere in between.....

Neither a wish as the stars fade away,
Neither a hope that the dawn brings a ray.
Neither in Love nor in Pain does she tread,
But in the quiet abyss where all words go dead.

7. Whispers of Memories

A love once tender, now weathered and torn.
It's a scent of Hatred that im tredding through
A wind too cruel to follow through,
Yet still its callous at my fragile heart.

The whispers of memories, soft as the night,
a tempest of longing, unyielding yet bright.
a haunting refrain that lingers on the skin,
Echoes of love, both fragile and broken,
Yet, in its embrace, I find where I've been.

So don't ask me where I'm going, too—
Even I no longer have a clue.

8. Empathy

The sky, once burdened with uncried tears,
Fell open, shedding all its fears.

As your empathy graced me,
The heavy clouds reckoned into melting waters......

9. End this Plight

What words do I write
And, end this plight
To convince,
The invincible me,
That,
you never loved me.

10. Mysterious Feeling

A mysterious feeling evolved, gushing
which I never experienced within
Where do these floods come from
from her eyes
flowing as incessant rains
roar up to my lips
like unwavering tides
this bittersweet ache,
a lover's refrain
And I named it as pain.....

11. Dream

Never there was a dream,
But I wander through the night,
Searching for your heartbeat,
In the fading, distant light.

Never there was a dream,
I saw you
When I see,
you hurt me there too....

12. You Always Remain Near Again

You are like a distant start,
Forgotten how it was to be near,
But,it seems the pain of you remained stagnant in my
eyes,
tears rolled down at once,
at the sight of you.....

Assuring, you were never distant,
you were never apart,
the tangled path where heartbeats reign,
Yet you always remain near again,
Though miles may stretch, and time may bend,

Reassuring every heartbeat, you transcend.
Yet you always remain near again.

13. Unnoticed Memoirs

Putting words to those unnoticed memoirs isnt easy
Where every pain has its own depth

Each tear dropped like ink, a story bled,
In silence, echoes of the things unsaid.
For every bruise holds a tale yet to mend,

Before those unnoticed memoirs were written
Those white pages were bruised red...

14. Ink of Pain

Those pale empty pages asking her
Not in Pain
Not in Love
Its ink of Pen
Or ink of Pain
she would be writing with ??

She would be writing with ,
Painful shadows of past.
Each word a weight, each line a scar,
Etched from pain buried within so far...

15. Unsaid Words

In those unsaid words
unwritten poems weaving again in my thoughts
Killing you in my words
giving life in few
some with love
some in Pain

Where each word bleed into memories
where each word etching with hope
where each word echoing the pain
difficult to breath, for every tear transcending in silence

No words were spoken, none were owed.
Just the warmth of being silently known.

16. Labyrinth of Pain

In a labyrinth of longing, endlessly I roam,
treading softly on the path of hope and despair,
waiting for the dawn to break, to set me free,
but still I wander, in this tapestry of ache.

Yet tangled in the whispers of hope,
She wandered once again,
Passing through these trenches of love,
She entered labyrinth of pain again,
Her heart a fragile compass, seeking paths unspent,
from where she could not come out ever again......

17. Weeping Skies

In shadows deep and languid,
where the old regrets reside,
She casts her fears like raindrops,
letting time be her guide.
Yet in the quiet corners,
where her weary spirit sighs,
She finds the seed of solace,
beneath the weeping skies.

18. Maze of Pain

I didn't run—I wandered in,
Where silence howled beneath the skin.
No signs to warn, no maps to read,
Just thorny paths that made me bleed.
Each turn a memory, sharp and bare,
And led me deeper, day by day.

A name was carved on every stone—
The ones I loved, the ones unknown.
They didn't stay, they didn't see
The maze they left inside of me.

But in that dark, I found a thread—
A single thought I almost said:
That pain may twist and wound and bend,
Mazes sometimes can come to an end.

19. Take Me Away

I am getting carried away in the arms of mother nature,
I am carrying more than my weight.
Mother nature,take me back in your womb
Shield me from the world's harsh noise,
Until my burdens can be laid down.
Take me away from all the Pain,
that i am yet to endure.....

20. Delicate Rose

She used to bloom where love had been,
Now petals fall from paper-thin skin.
She was a delicate rose
facing the cruel sun
She has become a dead rose
This bitterness, too cold to chart—
Is tearing me slowly,
drifting me apart.

On seeing a rainbow,
She hopes for a rain.
to fade that all Pain,
waiting for life to bloom again.

Oh so called Pain, shall never meet you again

21. End of Pain

At that very moment,
clock will be frozen
her last words will be inscribed in your heart forever
she would shed endmost tears of that longing pain
and,shall dissappear in the air.

And,you shall miss her
in the air you breathe...........